Norway's Best
(Cheese and Other Declicacies)

*To Mamma, Tante Solveig,
and Bestemor Olsen*

ACKNOWLEDGEMENTS

There are many people who contribute, often unaware, and over a period of time, to the completion of a book. For instance, from childhood I grew up around women who were good cooks, and who served nutritious and lovingly prepared food. They did not know when, nor did I, that they created memories for future generations.

Likewise, on my return visits to Norway, opportunities to sample the best in traditional Norwegian food created a curiosity within me which also contributed to this book. I wish to thank all you excellent Norwegian cooks, who, surely unwittingly, inspired me to keep Norwegian food traditions alive in America.

I deeply appreciate the assistance and liberal help of Anna-Karin Lindstad, Division Manager, Nutrition and Home Economics department, and Gyda Høye Horgen, Consultant, Norwegian Dairies Association. In addition to help with recipes, many sincere thanks for the use of the beautiful colored pictures in the center fold section of this book.

To my father-in-law, Melvin McCabe Scott, Sr. I am extremely grateful for his continual support, and especially for his efficiency in editing this work.

To Steve Andrist, Publisher, The Journal, I am truly grateful for his continuous assistance and encouragement.

I am thankful to Marleigh, (Martha Harrison) who's artistic work once more has made my work explicit.

I am grateful to my friend Lisa Matthews for her professional advice and help.

And to my husband Scotty, our children, their spouses, and my grandchildren, I am thankful for, and secure in your eternal love and reassurance.

Enthusiastically,

Astrid

Published by **Nordic Adventures**
7602 Holiday Valley Drive NW
Olympia, WA. 98502

ISBN 0-9634339-6-2
First Printing: May 1993

ASTRID KARLSEN SCOTT

Ekte Norsk Mat (Authentic Norwegian Cooking)
1976-1980-1983-1986-1991
Ekte Norsk Jul Vol. I (Traditional Norwegian Christmas) 1992
Norway's Fest Days 1993

Forthcoming Books:
Ekte Norsk Jul Vol. II (Traditional Christmas Foods)
Ekte Norsk Jul Vol. III (Traditional Christmas Songs and Stories)
Ekte Norsk Jul Vol. IV (Christmas Eve through New Year's Eve)
My Dear, Dear Kollen (Tulla's Island)

Copyright © 1993
by
Astrid Karlsen Scott

Printed in the Unites States by the Journal Publishing Company, Box E, Crosby, North Dakota 58730-0660. All rights reserved. No part of this work or its format covered by the copyright hereon may be reproduced or used in any form or by any means - graphic, electronic or mechanical, including photocopying, recording, taping or informational retrieval systems - without the written permission of the author.

NORWAY'S DAIRY INDUSTRY

Norway has some 348,000 milk cows and 64,000 goats. Together these animals keep 30,000 families employed. The dairy industry per se employs some 6,500 persons including those who work in research, laboratories, administration, sales, and transport. Each dairy is a cooperative society owned by the milk producers in the district. There are approximately 130 dairies in Norway today.

All milk producers, through their dairy, belong to Norway's National Milk Producer's Federation, NML. NML's priority is working for prize equalization throughout Norway. Another important work performed by NML is to instruct and guide the milk producers.

The Norwegian Dairy Association has the responsibility for marketing and sales of all Norway's Dairy Products both at home and abroad. It also oversees product planning and development, manufacturing and quality control.

The Norwegian Dairies' Testing Kitchen, serves as an information center where the consumers may receive information, and recipes on how to use the dairy products.

It is the generous help of the Norwegian Dairies Association, and their capeable staff, that made this book a reality.

CONTENTS

Acknowledgements 7

Norway's Dairy Industry 9

Velkommen to the world of Norwegian foods 13

Appetizers 15

Travel to the Mountain Farm 21

Visiting a Mountain Farm 23

Tradition Rich Cheeses 25

Warm Cheese Dishes and Sauces 37

Porridges and other Savory Tidbits 43

Traditional Milk Desserts 49

Waffles 55

Special Help 61

Credits 66

VELKOMMEN
—to the world of Norwegian foods!

Did you ever wonder what life would be like without cheese? The splendid world of Norwegian cheese? No goat cheese with waffles and *julekake*, or to add to sauces. No hot cheese fondues, cheese souffles, cheese casseroles, or cheese cake. Not even a *nøkkelost* sandwich, and no Jarlsberg with a juicy apple for an evening snack. Life without Norwegian cheese would be unthinkable, don't you agree?

Norway's food traditions are many and diverse, however. Like her protracted land varies with steep cliffs, and gentle valleys, deep fjords and rugged mountain plateaus, pristine lakes and cascading waterfalls, so the food has drawn its distinctive flavor from this rugged land the Norwegians cherish. The generous sea brings an abundance of food in exchange for diligent labors: sprats, salmon, herring, cod, haddock, halibut, pollack, flounder, and myriads of shellfish. From these the Norwegians make pickled herring, stockfish, *lutefisk*, smoked fish and the world's finest sardines and anchovies, to name a few.

Their surging rivers bring forth the brightly colored salmon. Marinated with the addition of dill it is known as the delectable *gravlaks*. The mountain trout which is at it's best in late August, the Norwegian's let it simmer ever so slowly in sour cream. Decades ago they learned to prepare *rakørret*, (half fermented trout), by keeping it cool, it can be enjoyed up to early February.

The meat from animals free to roam in rich pastures are not only tasty but have a high nutritional value. When one mentions, *spekeskinke* and *fenalår* it brings a smile to every Norwegian, so does Lamb and Cabbage, known as their national dish. Pork has always been a popular meat in Norway and there are numerous ways of preparing it, unique to Norway.

In their forests mushrooms, herbs, and berries grow in profusion. Tiny, wild strawberries, succulent raspberries, blackberries, blueberries, lingonberries, and in the mountain bogs grow the ultimate of all berries, *multer*, cloudberries; bursting with vitamin C, minuscule crunchy seeds, and the flavor of the mountain bogs from which they are gathered.

The Norwegians, never averse to hard work; in days passed gathered their families, pails and berry pickers, and headed for the woods for a day of harvesting berries and mushrooms. This is not as prevalent now as in earlier times, but I distinctly remember these novel days and how my parents made hard work into family days filled with frolic and unforgettable experiences, teaching their young ones to love and appreciate the abundance the land liberally offered. Ensuing the work, the reward; fresh succulent berries served with cream and sugar, accompanied by *pannekaker*, crepes, sprinkled with sugar and rolled up like a scroll, a traditional summer time treat. The remainder of the berries were made into fruit soups, juice, jam, or canned in water for the winter months ahead.

The mushrooms remembered best are the beautiful deep yellowish *kantarell*, chanterelle, they were easy to spot as they mostly grew in areas covered with moss, in between birch and pine trees. Not only were their beauty a delight to the eyes, but on arrival home when mamma slowly simmered them in a little butter, our enjoyment was complete.

In addition to the sampling of foods mentioned above, there are the nourishing porridges, breads and lefser, and the cookies made in unique cast iron forms.

Porridge it is maintained, is Norway's oldest, warm food dish, so are many of the milk and cheese recipes still used and enjoyed today. Accordingly, I will start this series of books concentrating on cheese, porridge, and other traditional dairy recipes. Many of these recipes have for generations, been part of the Norwegian food traditions, and I feel it is important that they are preserved.

Notwithstanding, included are also some of the latest recipes on how to enjoy the Norwegian cheeses to the fullest, complete with history, flavor and content.

Many of the recipes in this book are intended for fest days only, those days when food is meant to be memorable as well as the occasion. However, cheese is milk in concentrated form, and is chockfull of nourishment, and it is important that our bodies get their daily measure of health. Moreover, Norwegian cheese are among the finest and most flavorful in the world, so why not the best?

NORWAY'S BEST!

APPETIZERS
(Appetitt'vekkere)

Appetizers, when shared in a friendship or family circle, brings relaxation and enjoyment. It affords people an opportunity to unwind before the main meal, and it shows a caring host or hostess. In lives crowded with responsibilities it enhances the dinner hour, and the time allocated for enjoyment. It does not require an immense effort of time, nor means, only a little creativity. Cheese lends itself to appetizers, because of its adaptability to other foods, and because it is delicious served ungarnished as well. Create your own originals or try some of the recipes which follow. Many of the following recipes are a nice addition to a buffet table.

COCKTAIL SNACKS
(Pinnemat)

These snacks can be served by themselves or accompanied by flatbread, lefse, hardtack or crackers, and appropriate beverages. They add color and flavor to any table or get together. Attach the toothpicks with the snacks into fruits or vegetables, such as grapefruits, lemons, oranges, bright red apples, eggplant, cucumbers, or small red or white cabbages depending on the color and effect desired.

CHEESE AND SALMON
(Ost og laks)

¼ lb. smoked Norwegian salmon
¼ lb. Norwegian Swiss cheese
¼ cup sour cream, optional
½ tsp. dill
parsley

Cut cheese in ½" by 2" lengths. Cut salmon in rectangular slices. Mix sour cream and dill. Place cheese on salmon, spread lightly with sour cream. Place a tuft of parsley or dill in the center, roll up and fasten it all together with a toothpick. These appetizer are still very delicious if you omit the sour cream.

WALNUTS AND CHEESE
(Valnøtter og ost)

Walnuts taste excellent with cheese. Use cream cheese mixed with crushed, well drained pineapple.

Normanna or Roquefort has a piquant taste, try mixing them with a little cream or butter.

Walnuts halves
Normanna cheese (Norwegian Roquefort)
butter at room temperature
　　or light cream
small green grapes

Rub cheese through a sieve, or mash with a fork and blend with a little butter or cream. Place a small amount of cheese on whole walnut halves, press a grape into the cheese on one half and top with the other half. Attach a toothpick into the center and place into desired fruit. To give added color place fruit on bed of curly endive.

HAM AND CHEESE TIDBITS
(Skinke og ost appetittvekker)

Jarlsberg cheese
Ham
Fresh pineapple

Cube the cheese and cut slices of ham and fresh pineapple. Thread the cheese, then ham onto a toothpick and top with pineapple. Attach toothpick to desired fruit or vegetables.

SALAMI, CHEESE AND COCKTAIL ONION
(Salamipølse, ost og sylteløk)

The tiny cocktail onions are available in small glass jars and keep well.
Salami
Cheddar cheese
Cocktail onions

Fold salami slice in two, or fourth, depending on size. Thread on toothpick, followed by cheese. Top with one or two cocktail onions. Attach toothpick to desired fruit or vegetable.

MEATBALL SNACKS
(Kjøttkake pinnemat)

Make bitesize Norwegian meatballs. Attach to a toothpick. Add a small piece of marinaded, drained well, cucumber or small piece of Boston lettuce.

Marinade:
2/3 cup vinegar, white
2/3 cup water
4 tbsp. sugar
1/4 tsp. salt
dash of white pepper

Mix well and pour over Boston lettuce or thinly sliced cucumbers, preferably European. Make the marinade early enough to let dressing penetrate, about 1/2 hour before needed. It is popular in Norway to serve the marinated Boston lettuce and cucumbers as separate salads with meat or fish.

CHEESE TRAYS
(Ostebretter)

You can make some great cheese platters with fruit for an evening snack, a light supper, or desserts after a light buffet, or dinner.

You can serve cheese with *KJEKS*, a dry cookie or cracker, hardtack, or any kind of bread that does not clash with the cheese flavors. Vegetables such as celery, radishes, tomatoes, or cucumbers taste delicious with cheese. Or add fruit such as sliced apples, orange or tangerine wedges, kiwi fruit, pears or grapes. If you use apple slices or bananas, use a little lemon juice to prevent the fruit from darkening.

You need a minimum of two to three different kinds of cheese for just the two of you, or for several people you might want up to five or six different kinds of cheese. For example, Ridder, Brie, Jarlsberg, Norzola, goat cheese, and a typical dessert cheese. Among Norwegian-Americans, no matter what the occasion, there will be someone on the lookout for goat cheese. (See Tradition Rich Cheeses for definitions).

Choose cheese with different flavors and textures, something for everyone to enjoy.

Some soft cheeses come in their own little containers and look best in these, place them directly on the cheese tray. The hard cheese may be left in a whole piece or partly pre-sliced. Cut into logs and stack criss cross, or cube some of the cheeses and place in small clear glass bowls with toothpicks nearby.

When arranging a tray, take color and flavor into consideration. Strategically place the fruit or vegetables to be used in between the cheeses. Depending on the size of your platter you may add crackers, hardtack, or bread sticks directly to the platter. If you have several types, place on a separate platter or in a breadbasket with a colorful doily.

VARIOUS COCKTAIL SNACKS
(Varietet pinnemat)

There are numerous foods you can attach to toothpicks by themselves or in combinations and position into fruit or vegetables. You can use a combination of ingredients for example, Jarlsberg cheese and radishes, cocktail sausages broiled with a piece of bacon, or olives and cheese. Or thread separately, fresh small mushrooms, green or black olives, small pickles, berries or bits of fruit on to the toothpick. Attach all of one kind into a fruit or intermingle them so as to form a colorful pattern.

RIDDER APPETIZER
(Ridder appetitt vekker)

Beautiful, tasty, simple and easy.

Ridder cheese
Honeydew melon, ripe
Lemon juice
Mint leaves
Strawberries

Cut a long strip of Ridder cheese with cheese slicer. Fold it up like a rose. Slice 5 small wedges of honeydew melon, about 6/8" thick, and cut in half. Sprinkle with lemon juice and place like a pin wheel on a clear glass plate. Place your cheese flower in the center, and garnish with mint leaves and strawberries.

NORMANNA SOUP
(Normannasuppe)

The easiest of soups and flavorful, reminiscent of mushroom soup, but with more zest. Serve as appetizer before a light meal, or use for lunch with salad and good homemade bread.

4 oz. Normanna, grated
   (Norwegian Roquefort cheese)
2 tbsp. butter
2 tbsp. flour
3 cups bouillon, homemade beef broth,
   or 2 cans (14 1/2 oz.) Swanson
   Clear Beef Broth
1 cup sour cream
Parsley, chopped

Melt butter, stir in flour, and pour broth in all at once. stir until smooth. Let the soup simmer 5 minutes. Stir in sour cream until well blended. Pour into serving bowls add grated cheese and chopped parsley. 4 - 6 servings.

JARLSBERG VEGETABLE SOUP
(Jarlsberg grønnsaksuppe)

A marvelous first course soup, although it could be a meal in itself.
3 tbsp. butter
3 tbsp. flour
4 cups bouillon or beef broth
1 cup broccoli florets, app.
1 cup carrots, sliced
2 tbsp. chives
½ tsp. thyme
½ tsp salt
½ tsp. pepper
1 cup milk
8-9 oz. Jarlsberg

Melt butter, and stir in the flour. Pour in bouillon all at once, stir until smooth. Bring to a boil. Add remaining ingredients. Let simmer app. 8 minutes. Just before serving, stir in the grated cheese. 6-8 servings.

TRAVEL TO THE MOUNTAIN FARM
(Seterreise)

The *seter*, mountain farm, has always held some sort of magic for me. Here the mountain peaks seem to touch the sky, crisp mountain air fill my lungs, while the wide expanse of the minature world unfolds below.

However, dairy maids, whose day often lasted 16 hours, may not have enjoyed the mountain top views as much as I, a mountain hiker. And yet, I still hope for the time when I will have the experience of a few weeks on a mountain farm.

For a glimpse of what travel up to the *seter*, used to be, I have translated an excerpt from Hans Aanruds book, *Sidsel Sidserk*."

Across the valley a procession is working its way up the mountain path. Kjersti Hoel watches through the chamber window, following the procession with her eyes until they disappear over the grassy mountain side far into the interior of the mountain plateau.

"It is the livestock leaving for the *seter* today. *Budeia,* the dairy maid, lead, riding the *jegerhest*, Chasseur horse, dressed in her Sunday best, with a white kerchief, she rides high on the horse in a ladies saddle with a high frame resembling an arm chair. She is rosy, round, and self-asserting. Today she is in charge, and is the one who feels important.

"Following her are two fellows, each leading a horse positively straining under it's heavy burden. The livestock follows as in a grand parade. First, the lead cow, then Brandros with her crooked horn, then Krokhorn and Morkhei followed by other (except Farskall and Litage who remained at the farm in the valley to train the calves to follow). The large bull, as if to watch over all, comes last.

"The goats following the cattle closely, would love to pass them. Then the sheep in a close clump, followed by four large hogs. At the end are the assistant (second) dairy maid and Sidsel Sidserk with her filled rucksack. This is the first time Sidsel Sidserk was allowed to come to the *seter* with the cattle. From our childhood we had remembered we anxiously wondered if she could manage her job this summer...

(At the *seter*) "Sidsel Sidserk stood atop the turf covered roof ridge of the cow stable and scanned the view. With her birch bark hat, shepherd rucksack, goat horn bugle tied to a string around her neck, and her stick in hand she was ready for work...

"When summer ended, the animals penned inside the enclosure rambled impatiently about and understood that *bufarsdag,* the day for leaving the *seter*, had arrived. Laced panniers with butter and cheese tubs stood in a row. Horses loaded with panniers and packed saddles stood by the *seter* walls. In front stands the Chasseur horse with the lady saddle.

Men who herded the animals stood by with pipe in mouth waiting for the dairy maid busy making *bufars* cheese with the last milk, milked this morning which could not be left behind."

VISITING A MOUNTAIN FARM
(En setertur)

It is impossible for me to think of Norway in the summer time without thinking rømmegrøt, sour cream porridge. Like the summer my cherished friend, Else Aas, had heard of a mountain farm not too far from her family cottage at Gullverket; where we could buy fresh sour cream for our porridge. Else, Bjarne Nordli, another treasured friend, my sister Gro, and myself, drove a short distance, parked the car, and then started our hike into the mountains to find the little *seter*.

Our hike was slowed by picking the wild raspberries, blueberries, and lingonberries which grew in profusion, as if beckoning us to partake. The climb to the *seter* was beautiful and invigorating. As we made our ascent, the view below increased in magnificence, filling us with joy and anticipation to reach the *seter*.

We took a few wrong paths, after which the little mountain farm came into view. Mr. Soløst, it's friendly owner, a trump of a "homemaker," welcomed us.

His simple cottage had a living room, kitchen and bedroom. The sun shone brightly through spotless windows framed by checkered ourtains. And on the floor we admired the polished wood stove by a stack of logs, the ends cut evenly and appearing to be part of the wall. There also were a few unpretentious pieces of furniture in the room.

His small kitchen was filled with gleaming pans neatly arranged on wall racks, equipment to make butter, cheese and sour cream, a wood stove and small sink left just enough room for one or two people to turn around.

Mr. Soløst showed us around the *seter*, the chicken coop, and the barn for his sheep and 26 cows which was as clean as his cottage. After our "tour" he showed us how he made cheese, butter and his delicious sour cream. We bought two quarts of sour cream and began our decent.

Later, in the evening of the same day, we visited Bjarne's quaint cottage at Hol Lake. Bjarne is an expert *rømmegrøt* maker, and a lover of Norwegian food traditions. We watched by the lake the bright rays of the setting sun, while relishing every mouthful of Bjarne's steaming hot sour cream porridge, served with sugar, cinnamon, and black currant juice. And as we did, we sent grateful thoughts up to Mr. Soløst on his little summer mountain farm.

TRADITION RICH CHEESES
(Tradisjonsrike oster)

Norway is a cheese loving nation. In Norway, cows thrive on sparsely populated areas. By crystal clear rivers and unspoiled mountain sides they produce first grade milk for raw material all important in cheese making.

Our way of purchasing cheese at the supermarket, differs greatly from the days when the Norwegian dairy maids labored on the mountain farms from before sun up until late evening. In Anders Sandvig's book *Seterliv og Seterstell*, he says that the dairy maid's workday could last from 12 to 16 hours. Because her day began before dawn, it necessitated her getting to bed early, though this was not always feasible.

The cattle would often get to lick a few grains of salt from the dairy maids hand before she began the milking which took place in a shed or *utselet*, a building on the mountain farm.

She used wooden pails, which were made from pine, or juniper. The height of the bucket could be about 8" and the breadth between 12 to 13".

Usually bands made from hazel held the wooden staves together, seldom did they use iron for this. The pails had no handles, but a protruded pole to hold onto. Following the milking, the milk was strained through a wood strainer. In the center it had a round, cross shaped hole. A knitted hair strainer was placed in the center of this utensil and the milk then ran through the outlet hole. In later years the strainer was made from tin metal netting. If the milk was to be poured into a separate container they used a funnel also made from wood. After the containers were filled they placed these *melkekoller,* low milk bowls, on top of each other in 4 to 6 rows where they were left standing until they skimmed the cream off them. Many would place the *koller* on top of each other on a stone bench, in pyramid fashion.

It seems, in the olden days the milk was left standing a week before it was skimmed. By this time it would be quite sour, and thick, it would have consolidated and was viscous, and it could be skimmed off like a piece of skin. Then the cream stood another week before they began to churn the cream. In later years they began to churn the cream after 4-5 days. The left over sour milk was used in cooking or made into *gamalost* or other sour milk cheeses.

Gradually the cream was poured into the sour cream tubs. The sour milk was poured into *skjøkolken,* the sour milk container, there it would stand until they made cheese of it, or it was brought back into the valley on the pack horses.

Subsequently the dairy maid now had to clean the vessels used. First they all needed to be rinsed in lots of cold water from the streams. Then they were scrubbed inside out in warm water. Following which juniper branches were placed in the vessels and boiling water poured over, this was left standing until it cooled. The water was then poured out and the vessels were overturned onto cloth, ready for use the following morning.

The dairy maid's work continued through the day making rennet and the many different cheeses, and painstakingly preparing the food for other dwellers on the mountain farm.

When I contemplate on the work of the dairy maids, I cannot help but think how fortunate we are to be able to pick up almost any cheese we desire in a grocery store or a Scandinavian Delicatessen.

You may not live in an area where Norwegian cheeses are readily available, but many are now obtainable by mail in the USA. Knowing a little about them and their content will help you choose the proper cheese for the right dish.

GAMALOST
(Gamalost)

It has been said that the name *gamalost,* (old cheese) was the name given to the cheese because the old technique and method of making it had been handed down for generations. Other explanations are that since an abundance of newly made cheese was eaten in earlier times, and *gamalost* was the only cheese that was stored, it got its name because it was the oldest cheese on the farm.

Today *gamalost* is ready for sale within 5 weeks. It was, and is an art to make good *gamalost*. In the past hand skimmed milk was used, and special utensils and tools were needed. During the ripening process the cheese was kept in a chest or box which was only used for *gamalost*. Blessed the homemaker who had good *gamalost* mold in her coffer. This mold would be on the tools and in the chests for years. The storage temperature was important, and who knows, maybe the stories of some having kept the cheese in their straw mattresses were true.

Gamalost is not produced outside of Norway, yet the Norwegians have made *gamalost* for hundreds of years. It truly is a distinctive cheese and authentic Norwegian.

In days past nearly every farm and *seter* produced their own *gamalost*, but with the advancement of time, the imported cheeses made with rennet became more popular. The dairies took over the production of *gamalost* in the 1890's, the making of which is quite a sight.

The cultivated *gamalost* mold grows fast, and within a few days the cheese looks like huge, long haired balls of yarn. The mold is then brushed back into the cheese, and it ripens from the outside in, which is the reason the cheese is lighter in color toward the center and darker on the outer edges. The cheese should have a light golden color, be firm and moist and have a piquant appetizing flavor. If the cheese has an unpleasant odor it has become too ripe. The cheese should be kept cool, and well wrapped or in a covered cheese dish.

Serving gamalost: It is best sliced thin, preferably served on rye or any dark bread, maybe with an extra dab of butter.

Some use dark syrup with it, others spread a thin layer of honey on top, or a little lingonberry jam.

Lefser or flatbread makes a good accompaniment. Thin slices of *gamalost* with a little sour cream and good butter rolled up in a scroll is a delicacy. Remember! Gamalost is more than food, it is a part of the Norwegian culture.

SHARP, CREAMY CHEESE
(Pultost)

Pultost is also a very old cheese, and extremely easy to make. Made from soured skimmed milk or kefir, with the addition of caraway being the most popular. It is said that Norway has ten varieties of *pultost* with a thousand delicate distinctions. The cheese is known for being rich in protein and has a low fat content. Many feel it has not attained the acclaim it deserves. It is reasonable and goes along way. Served with butter on coarse bread it truly wakes up your appetite.

NORWEGIAN SWISS CHEESE
(Norsk Sveitserost)

In 1856, more than 150 years ago, when the first Norwegian Dairy, Rausjødalen Dairy, was established in Tolga, they hired a Swiss to head it. Being aware of the Swiss people's knowledge of cheese making, the Norwegians wanted to learn the very best method. The dairy's first year production consisted of 140 cheeses. Hundreds of Swiss came to Norway in the 1800's, they had a great influence on Norwegian cheese production in the beginning stages. It was only natural then that Swiss cheese would be among the first produced in Norway.

From that period until the 1950's the Norwegians made Swiss cheeses weighing 70 kilos. It was as big as a millwheel and extremely difficult to produce, as well as unwieldy. Finally the size was changed to the smaller Norwegian *sveitser* of today.

Of utmost importance in the production of Swiss cheese, is the quality of the milk. The cheese should have a firm consistency with large holes. Many believe if there is a drop of salt water in the holes, the cheese is fully ripe.

The Norwegian Swiss cheese is matured for at least 5 months. By then the sweet nutlike flavor characteristic to Swiss cheese is developed. The Norwegian Swiss cheese is above all intended for sandwiches and cheese trays, but may also be used in cheese dishes. In fondue for example, this Swiss cheese is tops.

GOUDA-TYPE NORVEGIA CHEESE
(Goudatype Norvegia ost)

Norwegian cheese of the gouda type have in the last few years been named Norvegia, speaking of both the one without rind and the little round mini Norvegia with rind. The Norvegia is loved in most Norwegian homes and used daily. Norvegia's ancestors hailed from Holland. It obtained its name from the town of Gouda in southern Holland. Since those early days it has gone through innumerable changes, and one can safely say that the Norvegia of today is a typical Norwegian cheese. It has a mild, but rich flavor with a pliant consistency, and has small even "eyes".

In Norwegian homes it is above all others, known as the "sandwich cheese", and is included both on the breakfast table, in the lunch pack and for evening snacks. And today, the youth enjoy it on a pizza, yes indeed, times have changed.

JARLSBERG
(Jarlsberg)

Most of the Norwegian cheeses have forerunners in foreign lands. Jarlsberg is genuine Norwegian. This distinguished, world renowned cheese is of a soft, pliable texture and has a mild nut like flavor making it excellent for cooking and in salads.

This cheese was first produced in the early 1800's on the old Jarlsberg estate, its namesake, on the western shore of the Oslofjord.

Difficult times and reasonable cheese imported from Holland abated the cheese production at Jarlsberg. Nontheless, its reputation and unusual qualities was not forgotten over these years, and more than 100 years later the cheese specialists at Norway's Agricultural School, under the direction of Professor Ola Martin Ystgaard set out to reconstruct the Jarlsberg cheese. It took several years and hundreds of experiments before Professor Ystgaard would allow the cheese on the market in the early 1960's. Anyone who has tasted the exquisite Jarlsberg cheese knows Professor Ystgaard succeeded with his goal. The cheese is exported around the world as well as thoroughly enjoyed at home in Norway. Cheese experts worldwide have searched for the secret, but so far in vain.

Jarlsberg is made into 10 kilo round wheels with rind, and rind free cheeses. Foremost it is a marvelous party and sandwich cheese, but lends itself remarkably well to warm cheese dishes.

EDAM CHEESE
(Edamerost)

Originally this cheese came from the town of Edam, Holland. It is round, it is said, because in days of old they used to roll the cheese in small wooden chutes onto the ships which transported them around the world.

The Norwegian Edam cheese has become the Christmas cheese and fest cheese for important celebrations in Norway. It has a mild, rich and a refreshing piquant taste. It keeps well under controlled temperature.

It takes 4 months to prepare Edam cheese. The homemakers in olden days began the preparations for their Christmas cheese in August, 4 months ahead. Today it still takes 4 months to produce Edam cheese, but homemakers buy them in the stores except for rare exceptions. Cut the Edam cheese in layers, in little triangles from the top down. It tastes best thickly sliced, and is delicious with grapes.

NØKKELOST
(Nøkkelost)

In times past when *nøkkelost* was imported from Holland, the cheese factory in Leyden stamped the city emblem, two crossed keys on it, hence the name *nøkkelost,* or Key cheese. Today the *nøkkelost* made in Norway is typical Norwegian. The dairies began producing them as early as the middle of last century. Since then there have been many renditions and variations.

The Norwegians think of the *nøkkelost* as an every day cheese, but with what flair! It is delicious on an openface sandwich, served on dark bread and accompanied with fruit. The cheese is elegant used in cooking. Its aromatic spices of cumin and cloves, opens the door wide for any creative cook. Try it in salads, sauces, souffles or cakes. It's unique flavor is loved by everyone.

The Americans, in time, insisted on a softer and more pliant cheese. The Norwegians solved the problem by making a gouda type cheese with the *nøkkelost* spices. This delicious cheese now has gained popularity in Norway as well. The *nøkkelost* matures for three months before it appears in the grocery stores.

NORMANNA
(Normanna)

Norway's *Normanna,* is somewhat similar to the french Roquefort cheese, both in flavor and looks. Originally one would allow mildew to grow on slices of *loff,* a white bread similar to french bread. The bread would then be dried, crushed and added to the cheese containers. Today, the fungus needed is cultivated and added. The cheese is made from cow's milk. It has a sharp aromatic taste. A versatile cheese, it is appetizing both as a sandwich spread and as an addition to soups, sauces, lamb chops, and in salads. As a snack with red grapes, radishes, and celery it is tops. On a buffet or in cheese trays it is a must.

RIDDER CHEESE
(Ridder Ost)

This is a true aristocrat. *Ridder* literally means knight, it is a cheese for our times. Created for those who relish a generous slice of cheese. It is produced from rich, high quality milk in a small dairy by one of the most beautiful fjord-arms in Norway.

It came on the market in the late 60's, is round and approximately 8 inches in diameter. Weighs about 3 lbs. It is surface ripened for 5-6 weeks and has a soft texture.

Ridder is a distinctive dessert cheese. When served, *Ridder* should be accompanied with the season's berries and fruits, such as strawberries, kiwi, and ripe grapes.

The cheese gets it's full aroma at room temperature, and has an aromatic, piquant flavor, and should be cut with a sharp knife.

TILSITER
(Tilsiter)

The Belgian Limberger cheese is thought to be the forerunner to the *Tilsiter* cheese now produced in many countries. The original went to Holland, Germany and Austria. Some Dutch emigrants brought the cheese with them to East Prussia, among the emigrants there was a lady who made a cheese she named after Tilsit, the town in which they settled.

The production of Norwegian *Tilsiter* began in the 1950's when the opportunity presented itself to export cheese to Germany and the continent, including Holland. The production of *Tilsiter* was started because it was a cheese much loved in many countries. Before the European import restrictions started Norway produced some 2000 ton of *Tilsiter* yearly, half of which was exported.

The Norwegian *Tilsiter* differs from the Norvegia in that it is more pliant, and of a very different texture. It is by covering the cheese with a special culture during the ripening process which gives it it's unique flavor. It is a marvelous cheese for sandwiches, lends itself well to be served with milder cheeses on cheese trays. It has a strong aroma and is therefore not suitable in warm dishes.

GOAT CHEESE
(Gjetost)

The Norwegian Dairy Association says *gjetost* is as native to Norway as trolls and fjords. It all started, they say, more than 100 years ago on a small summer farm high up from the Gudbrandsdal valley, famous for it's rich farming traditions. The milk maid had just made the curd cheese from cow's and goat's milk. The left over whey was boiling in a great iron kettle in the fire place.

Usually she would allow almost all the liquid to evaporate. The golden paste that was left at the bottom of the kettle, was used for sandwich spread. A particular night she expected visitors and wanted to serve them something special. She added cream and some goat milk and poured the hot mixture into a mold. Unbeknown to her, that night she probably served the very first golden *gjetost* ever made. This is how the sweet golden *gjetost* became the staple breakfast treat in every Norwegian home.

Today *gjetost* still is made the same way, but modern techniques and equipment have taken over. The Norwegians' appetite for goat cheese, however, is insatiable.

As children in Norway we were all fed school breakfasts. In memory, they never varied. A glass of milk, *skonrok*, a hard roll or hardtack, or a course dark rye bread with *gjetost*, and an apple or orange. Every morning it tasted just as delicious, especially when in the freezing winter mornings we entered heated schoolrooms, with our breakfasts ready for us on the school desk.

The *gjetost* is a 100% natural product, no sugar or color is added. The sweetness comes from the milk sugar caramelizing when cooked.

Remember to serve the cheese in wafer thin slices. Here, nothing but a Norwegian cheese slicer will do, (you need one anyway) available in any Scandinavian shop, or fine department stores.

▲ Cheese in a summer garden.　　　　　　　　Cheese makes any event extraordinary. ▼

▲ Nøkkelost Quiche

Dessert Cheese ▼

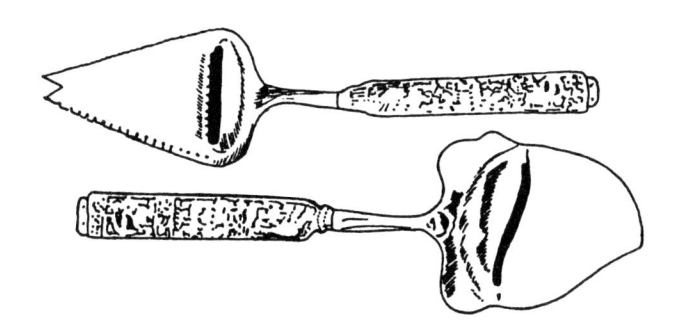

CARE OF THE CHEESE
(Ta vare på osten)

Cheese keeps well, but certain guidelines should be followed. A cheese which is vacuum packed keeps for about 2 months. Never keep several kinds of cheese together in one package as they will take on the different flavors. Wrap tightly and with care. Air, moisture and acid causes mold to appear.

Mold should be cut off, and the cheese wrapped in new foil. White cheese should not be frozen, the texture is easily destroyed. Shredded cheese, however, lends itself to freezing. Wrap in small portions. Cream cheeses, *gamalost* and Normanna freezes well.

All cheese tastes best when close to room temperature.

Keep in mind that cheese is a superb food product to have in reserve.

WARM CHEESE DISHES AND SAUCES
(Varme osteretter og sauser)

NØKKELOST SAUCE
(Nøkkelost saus)

3 tbsp. butter
3 tbsp. flour
1 ½ cup milk
½ tsp. salt
½ tsp. Dijon mustard
3 cups nøkkelost, grated
ham, chopped

Melt butter in saucepan. Stir in flour. Pour milk in all at once and stir until smooth and thick. Simmer 5 minutes. Season with salt and mustard. Add cheese, stirring until melted. Serve over fresh cooked vegetables sprinkled with cooked ham. Serves 4.

GAME SAUCE
(Tradisjonell Viltsaus)

2 tbsp. butter
2 tbsp. flour
1 cup bouillon
1 cup sour cream
½ cup 100% goat cheese, diced
3 juniper berries
2 tsp. salt
1 tsp. pepper, freshly ground

Brown butter and flour in an iron frying pan. Add bouillon and sour cream at once. Stir over medium heat until smooth and bubbly. Add diced cheese and spices. Let simmer 10 minutes. If a darker color is desired, add a little Maggi seasoning.

GOAT CHEESE GRAVY FOR CHICKEN OR GAME
(Geitost saus til vilt)

5/8 cup goat cheese or Gudbrandsdalost, diced
1 ⅓ bouillon
1 cup sour cream
½ tsp. pepper
6-8 juniper berries, crushed

Melt goat cheese in one third of the bouillon. Add remaining bouillon, bring to a boil. Lower heat, add sour cream under constant stirring and let simmer 4-5 minutes until desired consistency. Add pepper and juniper berries to taste.

OLD FASHIONED SAUCE
(Gammaldags duppe)

3/8 cup 100% goat cheese, grated
2 2/3 cup water
1/4 cup flour
1/3 cup sugar
1/3 cup sour cream, good measure

Grate cheese and bring to boil with 2 cups water. Stir flour into remaining water until smooth, add to cheese with sugar, and stir until it begins to boil. Let simmer 10 minutes, stirring occasionally. Add sour cream. Serve with *klubb* (large dumplings).

SOUR CREAM GRAVY
(Rømmesaus)

Tasty with chicken, veal or game.
1 1/8 cup sour cream or
    sour cream light
3/8 cup goat cheese, grated
1/3 cup chives, parsley or dill

Over medium heat stir cheese and sour cream until melted. Stir in finely chopped greenery. Delicious with chicken or game.

NØKKELOST QUICHE
(Nøkkelostpai)

5/8 cup butter
7/8 cup flour
2 tbsp. water
Filling:
6 slices bacon
2/3 cup mushrooms, fresh or canned
4 eggs, slightly beaten
1 cup whipping cream
1 cup *nøkkelost*, grated
1/2 tsp. salt
1/2 tsp. white pepper

Cut butter into flour. Add water and mix to soft dough. Press into a 9 1/2" quiche pan. Fry bacon until crisp and break into pieces. Fry mushrooms in a little of the bacon fat. Mix bacon and mushrooms with remaining ingredients and pour into pie shell in quiche pan. Bake until firm, on the lowest rack in the oven at 350 degrees.

NØKKELOST OMELETTE
(Nøkkelost omelett)

3 tbsp. butter
6 eggs
6 tbsp. water
½ tsp. salt
2 ½ cups nøkkelost, grated
3 red or yellow bell peppers, chopped
1 ¼ cup cooked ham, sliced
Parsley, chopped

Melt butter in skillet. In a bowl beat together eggs, water and salt. Pour into skillet. Sprinkle cheese evenly onto the omelette mixture. Sprinkle peppers on top. Cook covered over moderate heat until eggs are set and cheese is melted, 8-10 minutes. Do not stir. Serve immediately, sprinkled with parsley, and accompanied with ham. 4-6 servings

NØKKELOST VEGETABLE CASSEROLE
(Nøkkel grønnsakform)

1 medium eggplant, sliced
2 medium zucchini, sliced
⅜ cup oil
1 cup fresh mushrooms, sliced
2 small leek, sliced thinly
1 small green pepper, cut in strips
10-12 cherry tomatoes, or an equal amount of tomato slices
1 tsp. salt
½ tsp. pepper
1 cup nøkkelost, grated

Brown eggplant and squash lightly in a little oil. Add mushrooms, leek, pepper, tomatoes, salt and pepper. Place grated cheese and vegetables in layers in an ovenproof casserole, ending with cheese on top. Bake in 350 degree oven until cheese is melted, about 20 minutes.

JARLSBERG VEGETABLE LASAGNA
(Jarlsberg grønnsaklasagne)

Vegetable mixture:
4 tbsp. butter or oil
2 lg. onions, sliced
3 carrots, sliced
1 cup celery, diced
1 cup tomatoes, chopped
1 cup mushrooms, sliced
1 bay leaf

Cheese sauce:
3 tbsp. butter
3 tbsp. flour
2 ¾ cup milk
2 cups Jarlsberg, grated

oregano
salt and pepper
lasagna

Fry onions, carrots and celery in butter. Add remaining ingredients. Let simmer 15 minutes. Cook lasagna according to directions on package. Make a white sauce from butter, flour and milk, simmer 8 minutes. Add Jarlsberg stir until melted. Arrange layers of lasagna and vegetables mixture in ovenproof casserole. Cover with cheese sauce. Bake at 350 degrees 40 minutes. 4-6 servings.

JARLSBERG COD
(Jarlsberg torsk)

2 lbs. cod fillet
1 tbsp. butter
1 tsp. salt
½ tsp. white pepper
1 clove garlic, minced

1 small leek, thinly sliced
3 tomatoes, small
1 ¾ cup Jarlsberg, grated
⅔ cup half and half

Clean and dry fish. Cut into serving size portions and place in a greased shallow baking dish. Season with salt, pepper and garlic. Arrange sliced leek and tomato slices over fish. Top with cheese and pour half and half over all. Bake in 350É oven until done. Serves 4-6.

JARLSBERG FILLED PEPPERS
(Jarlsbergfylt paprika)

4 large peppers, red or green
2 tsp. coarse salt
1 lb. ground meat, low fat
½ tsp. Tabasco
½ tsp. garlic salt
½ tsp. pepper, coarsely ground

Juice of 1 lemon
⅔ cup French bread crumbs
1 ¼ cup Jarlsberg, diced
¼ cup butter, scant
garlic salt

Divide peppers in two, remove stem and seeds. Sprinkle the coarse salt on baking pan. Mix meat, Tabasco, garlic salt, pepper, lemon juice, crumbs, and half of Jarlsberg cheese. Divide evenly between the peppers. Top the peppers with remainder of the cheese. Melt butter, add garlic salt and brush over the peppers. Place on top of coarse salt on baking sheet, and bake in 350 degree oven about 35 minutes. Serves 4-6.

NORVEGIA FILLED POTATOES
(Norvegiafylte poteter)

4 baking potatoes
6-8 slices bacon
1 cup Norvegia, grated
2 small onions, diced
1 egg

2 tbsp. green pepper, diced
2 tbsp. red pepper, diced
salt & pepper
sour cream & chives

Bake the potatoes till almost done. Cut in two and remove most of the inside. Fry bacon until crisp and break in pieces. Mix potato with bacon, cheese, (save a little to sprinkle on top), onion, egg, peppers, salt and pepper. Fill the shells and sprinkle cheese on top. Put potatoes back in the oven and let bake until warm throughout (about 15 minutes), and cheese is melted. Serve with sour cream and chives, and a nice green salad.

NORVEGIA SPINACH PIE
(Norvegia spinatpie)

Filling:
2 cups chopped spinach, frozen and thawed
7 slices bacon
2/3 cup Norvegia
1 1/3 cup milk
3 eggs
1 tsp. salt
1/2 tsp. nutmeg, grated

Pie dough:
7 tbsp. butter
2/3 cup flour
1 tbsp. water

Make a regular pie dough, set to cool. Place spinach in a sieve and drain all water. Fry bacon until crisp, and crumble.

In a bowl slightly beat the milk, eggs, salt and nutmeg together. Line a 9" pie plate with pastry. Trim 1/2" beyond rim and tuck under. Flute edges. Spoon spinach into pie shell, add bacon and shredded cheese. Pour egg mixture over. Bake in moderate oven, 350 degrees 30-40 minutes or till knife inserted halfway between center and edge comes out clean. Serve warm.

SWISS OR NORVEGIA CHEESE SOUFFLE
(Ostegrateng)

1 1/3 cup whole milk
4 tbsp. flour
1 1/4 cup cheese, grated Norwegian Swiss or Norvegia

4 eggs
1 tsp. salt

Make a smooth thickening from milk and flour. Bring to a boil in a saucepan. Add cheese and let melt over low heat while stirring. Cool and add beaten eggs and salt. Pour into ungreased souffle dish. Bake at 350 degrees for 50-60 minutes. Serve immediately. Serve with French bread and green salad.

LAMB CHOPS WITH NORMANNA CHEESE
(Lammekoteletter med Normannaost)

The Normanna cheese, similar to French roquefort in flavor, adds a new and exciting taste to lamb chops.

Lamb chops
Normanna cheese
Brussels sprouts

Canned peaches
Currant jelly

Nicely brown, on both sides, as many lamb chops as needed. When done, add a couple of slices of Normanna cheese to each chop, and let slowly simmer until cheese is melted. Remove the chops to warm serving platter. Placing them in the center, with brussels sprouts along one side, and halved peaches with a dab of currant jelly in the center, along the other side.

SWISS CHEESE AND GREEN BEANS
(Sveitser og grønne bønner)

These appetizing green beans can be a meal all of its own, or as a compliment to meats.

2 tbsp. flour
1 cup sour cream
1 tsp. onion, finely chopped
¼ tsp sugar
1 tsp. salt
2 lbs. fresh green beans,
    frozen or canned, cooked
1 cup Swiss cheese, grated
½ cup almonds, slivered

Make a thickening of flour and sour cream. Bring to a boil, over medium heat, while stirring constantly, add onion, sugar and salt. Place beans and cheese in layers in an oven proof casserole or divide equally into individual casseroles. Poor the sauce over. Sprinkle with slivered almonds. Bake in 350 degree oven until hot and cheese is melted.

PORRIDGES AND OTHER SAVORY DELIGHTS
(Grøt og andre lekkerbisken)

SOUR CREAM PORRIDGE
(Rømmegrøt)

Rømmegrøt, sour cream porridge, has always held a *hedersplass*, - in high esteem, in Norwegian food culture. It was and in many places still, is used at celebrations to commemorate certain days.

In the past, though the recipes were similar, the porridge was given different names like *slåttegraut*, usually served to celebrate the end of haying. It was customarily cooked with thick sour cream, and served with flatbread and milk. Or if the porridge was served the day the cattle were moved to or from the summer mountain farm, it was called *bufarsgraut*. Some used *dravle*, simmered curds and whey. The dairy maid either cooked the porridge at the seter or on her return to the farm. The curds and whey served as an accompaniment, were always prepared at the summer farm. Even at weddings and at births the sour cream porridge was a welcome *sending*, contribution.

These offerings would arrive in intricately carved, or rosepainted wooden vessels made especially for the porridge, and delighted and nourished the happy recipients. The porridge itself, in some areas, was decorated with diamond shapes of sugar and cinnamon.

Rømmegrøt was a must for Midsummer festivities, June 24th, and for Olsok, July 29th, this holds true as well to day. Today it is usually served with *spekemat*, salt-cured smoked meat, and flatbread as accompaniments.

Rømmegrøt is a heavy meal, but our forefathers, whose day began before sun up and continued long past sun down, were more concerned with nourishment than calories. The porridge is not recommended for everyday use, but rather to be saved for celebrating special days.

Rømmegrøt cannot be made in a hurry - patience is the key to success. Ingredients used must be the very best quality.

Today much of the butter fat, a necessary ingredient for this porridge, has been removed from the cream. If sufficient butter does not ooze out while cooking, supplement with 2 to 3 tablespoons of unsalted butter.

The first recipe included is an old recipe for the more experienced and adventuresome cook. However, keep in mind that our processed commercial cream will not sour properly by standing at room temperature, and therefore may not prove satisfactory. Non-commercial sour cream is best for this method. All recipes, however, require patience and constant stirring.

SOUR CREAM PORRIDGE I
(Rømmegrøt)

Keep desired amount of fresh whipping cream at room temperature for a couple of days to sour. Pour into a heavy-bottomed kettle, simmer over low heat about 10 minutes. Begin to sift the flour, a little at a time, stirring constantly with a wooden spoon, until it becomes a thick mass and leaves the sides of the pan. Continue stirring and cooking until the butter begins to ooze out from the cream/flour mixture. If no butter separation occurs, add one to two tablespoons of unsalted butter. Depending on the quality of cream used, the butter might begin to show immediately, but often it takes up to 10 minutes or longer. As soon as the butter begins to ooze skim off immediately with spoon and reserve in a separate, small pan. Remove all of it as there is still plenty of fat remaining in the porridge. When all the butter has been removed, continue stirring, and sift in as much flour as the porridge can possibly hold. Add boiling milk, 1 tablespoon at a time, stirring constantly. Continue adding milk until of proper consistency. Add salt to taste. When all the milk has been added bring to a quick boil and remove from heat. Serve *rømmegrøt* with sugar, cinnamon, and a generous *smørøye* ("eye" of butter) using that which was removed from the porridge during cooking. When preparing large amounts of *rømmegrøt* it may be necessary to melt additional butter. Serve delicious fresh currant or raspberry juice as an accompanying beverage. Some people prefer milk with *rømmegrøt*, but I feel that a refreshing fruit drink is a must with such a rich, though delectable porridge.

In certain places in Northern Norway they serve their *rømmegrøt* with a little grated mild goat cheese.

SOUR CREAM PORRIDGE II
(Rømmegrøt II)

This cannot be made with our commercial sour cream which is processed to prevent butter separation, which is so essential to the dish. If non-commercial sour cream is not available, make your own as described below.

2 cups heavy cream, or non-commercial sour cream
2 tbsp. lemon juice
1 cup flour
½ tsp. salt
2 cups hot milk

(This is a minimum amount. You could need as much as 1 cup more to achieve proper consistency.)

Pour cream into saucepan and stir in lemon juice. Let stand for 15 minutes. Bring cream to a boil and simmer gently for 5 minutes. Sprinkle with ½ cup of the flour and blend thoroughly. Continue cooking for 10 minutes or more, or until butter comes to the surface. Beat constantly. According to your taste the butter may stay in the porridge, or you may skim it off and keep hot in a separate pan. When no more butter oozes from the mixture, under constant stirring, sprinkle in the remaining flour. Add hot milk a tablespoon at a time, stirring constantly until porridge is thickened and smooth. Salt mildly to taste. Serve hot, with butter, sugar and cinnamon.

SOUR CREAM PORRIDGE FROM TINE
(Rømmegrøt fra Tine)

2 cups water
5/8 cups butter
1 qt. whipping cream
2 cups kefir
1 egg
1 2/3 cup flour or more (1/4 cup
   or more should be barley flour
   mixed with the white flour)
2 tsp. salt

In a heavy-bottomed kettle bring water and butter to a boil. Whisk together cream, kefir and egg. Pour into water mixture while stirring. Simmer for 15 minutes while stirring frequently. Sift in flour while beating constantly. Let simmer for another 10 minutes. Beat constantly. After a few minutes butter will separate from porridge. Skim off butter and save in a small bowl, keeping it hot. Add salt to porridge. Serve the porridge with sugar and cinnamon. Pass melted butter for those who would not think of eating the porridge without it. Enjoy with red berry juice or milk.

SOUR CREAM PORRIDGE FROM HARDANGER
(Rømmegrøt fra Hardanger)

In this old recipe, cream of wheat is used to cut down on its richness. Do not use instant cream of wheat.

1/3 cup cream of wheat, non-instant
3 cups skim milk
3 cups sour cream, non commercial
2 tbsp. flour, app.
2/3 cup barley flour, scant
3/4 tsp. salt

Cook the cream of wheat with the skim milk according to direction on package. Set aside. Make your sour cream porridge of flour and sour cream as for Harvest Sour Cream Porridge. While stirring add a little of the cooked cream of wheat at a time. Bring to a boil between each addition. Allow to simmer 10 minutes after the last addition, stirring continually. Butter will begin to ooze out but keep it in the porridge. Add salt. Serve piping hot with sugar, cinnamon and berry juice, smoked sausage, flatbread or *vannkringler*.

HARVEST SOUR CREAM PORRIDGE
(Slåttegraut)

1 ½ qt. heavy cream or half sweet and half sour cream
1 cup unbleached or barley flour, or ½ cup of each
½ tsp. salt

If you use all whipping cream, the porridge will be extremely heavy. It is better to use half sweet and half sour cream. Boil the porridge in an iron kettle if possible. Gently let the cream simmer for 10 minutes. Sprinkle the flour into the cream while stirring vigorously. Continue to let the porridge simmer until the butter oozes out, beating continually. This could take another 10 minutes or more. Add salt. Do not remove the butter, but serve porridge as is with the butter floating on top. Serve with raspberry, currant or lingonberry juice.

RICE PORRIDGE
(Risgrynsgrøt)

1 ⅔ cups water
⅔ cup rice, long grain
4 cups milk, boiling
1 ½ tbsp. butter
Salt and sugar to taste
Cinnamon

Sprinkle rice into the boiling water, and stir until boiling. Cover and cook slowly until most of the water has been absorbed. Add boiling milk, stir, and continue to simmer until rice is tender and porridge has thickened. Total cooking time about 1 ½ hour. Add butter and salt. Serve hot, with milk, sugar and cinnamon. Serves 4.

PARTY RICE PORRIDGE
(Festrisgrøt)

Use same recipe as above, omitting butter, and substituting 2 cups of sour cream for two cups of the milk. Add the sour cream when the porridge has thickened. Bring to a boil stirring continually. Add the salt. Serve hot, with milk, sugar and cinnamon.

BOILED MILK FOR DUMPLINGS
(Bollemelk)

Dumplings boiled in milk is an old Norwegian favorite. They vary according to different sections of the country: some are made with butter and flour, some with potatoes etc. In a heavy bottom kettle, simmer desired amount of milk with a stick of cinnamon and a pinch of salt. Set aside, add dumplings.

DUMPLINGS
(Klot)

1 2/3 cup flour
5/8 cup milk
1/2 tsp cardamon
1/2 tsp salt
1 egg, slightly beaten

Make a smooth thick batter from flour and milk. Allow to rest one half hour. Add spices and egg. Fill a tablespoon three quarter full with batter and shape dumplings against the edge of a bowl. Carefully place in the warm milk. Let simmer over low heat 10 minutes. Be careful not to scorch milk. See MILK in Special Help section.

TELEMARK GOMME
(Telemark gomme)

Gomme is a much enjoyed traditional dish. This too varies somewhat in the various districts. It is used as an accompaniment to waffles and *lefser*. This unique *gomme* from Telemark requires a lot of stirring, but with our electric beaters it is well worth the effort. The finished *gomme* will have a delicious and unusual creamy consistency.

6 qts. milk
6 eggs
1/2 cup brown sugar

Bring the milk to the boiling point while stirring continually. Pour into a separate casserole with a heavy bottom and let it simmer uncovered for approximately 5 hours. Gently shake the pan periodically. Do not remove the coating, *snerken*, which will form on top of the milk. The *gomme* will now have the consistency of a thick sauce and have a light golden color. At high speed beat eggs and sugar together in a bowl. Add the boiled milk, a few table spoons at a time, while continually beating at a high speed. When all milk is added, continue to beat on low until the *gomme* is lukewarm. Enjoy with waffles and lefse. There is plenty here to share as well.

SIMMERED CURDS AND WHEY
(Dravle)

This *dravle* dish comes from the county of Rogaland. Chill thoroughly. Serve as an accompaniment to waffles and *lefser*. Eat with a spoon.

2 qts. milk
7/8 cup whipping cream
2 cinnamon sticks
2 2/3 cup kefir
1/2 cup sugar, scant
5 eggs

Bring milk, cream, and cinnamon sticks to a boil. Whip kefir, sugar and eggs together and add to milk mixture under constant stirring. Gradually remove 1/3 of the whey as it separates from the curds. Stir carefully and let *dravlen* simmer for about 1 hour or until ready. Chill thoroughly. Serve as an accompaniment for waffles and lefser.

CREAMY, SHARP CHEESE
(Pultost)

Pultost has many variations. You choose the flavor. Caraway is what I remember best, but dill, chives or leek is also delicious.
 1 quart kefir, or unflavored non-fat yogurt
 4 tbsp. sour cream
 ½ tsp. salt
 Seasoning or herbs
In a heavy saucepan over low heat, heat the milk or yogurt until it separates, it is very important to let it do so slowly. Do not stir. Strain the cheese mass through double cheese cloth placed in a sieve over a bowl. When most of the whey has drained off, pick up the four corners of the cheese cloth and squeeze out the remainder. Do not discard the whey, but use in bread-baking or as a healthy drink. Place the cheese in a bowl and add sour cream and seasoning of your choice. I use 4 tablespoons of caraway to a quart, you might want to use less. Let the cheese stand for 24 hours to develop flavor. Keeps in covered container in refrigerator for up to two weeks.

EGG CHEESE
(Egg ost)

This *eggost* comes from West Agder. Though it is a cheese, it is served with sugar and cinnamon. It is simple to make and tasty.
 1 qt. milk
 6 eggs
 1 cup sugar
 1 cup kefir or cultured milk
In a heavy pan bring the milk to a boil. Let cool slightly. Beat eggs, sugar and cultured milk together. While stirring vigorously pour the egg mixture, a little at a time, into the warm milk, and bring to a boil. (Strain off the whey, and use in your bread baking.) Serve with sugar and cinnamon.

MOUNTAIN DAIRY MAID'S FAVORITE
(Seterjentas favoritt)

Use this spread on your favorite *lefser*, waffles, or hard rolls. Delicious!
 ⅞ cup butter
 ⅞ cup 100% goat cheese
 ¼ cup powdered sugar, scant
 1 tsp. cardamom
Stir butter until soft. Grate cheese, add to butter. Add powdered sugar & cardamom.

TRADITIONAL MILK DESSERTS
(Tradisjonelle desserter)

For ages, desserts made with milk, soured milk or cream were a common, and welcome, nutritious dessert in Norway. Some of the most popular are included here. The Caramel, Rum and Cream of wheat pudding are, of course, of later origin, but have been very popular in the 20th century.

DESSERT CHEESE
(Kokaost)

A tasty side dish with homemade waffles and *lefser*. So simple to make, and so nourishing.

2 ½ qt. whole milk
1 qt. kefir or cultured milk
1 small egg, or a half one
⅔ cup raisins
sugar & cinnamon

Bring the milk to the boiling point. Beat egg and kefir together and add to milk while stirring. Let stand until whey separates from the cheese mass. Strain well through a cheesecloth placed in a strainer. Press the cheese into a mold or spring-form pan, with layers of raisins in between. Sprinkle sugar and cinnamon on top. See picture page 34.

SUMMER COLD DISH
(Sommerkoldtskål)

⅔ cup whipping cream
1 qt. cultured milk or kefir
Juice of ½ lemon
3 tbsp. sugar
1 tsp. vanilla
Thin slices of lemon
3 tbsp. almonds, coarsely chopped
Strawberries
Rusks

Whip cream. Carefully stir in kefir. Add lemon juice, sugar and vanilla sugar. Pour into a large bowl. Cover and chill thoroughly - possibly in the freezer for awhile. When ready to be served, decorate with lemon slices and serve with fresh strawberries and rusks.

CRUMBLED FLATBREAD IN KEFIR MILK
(Flatbrødsoll)

Many traditional milk recipes started on the mountain farms. The dairy maids were ingenious in using the animals milk.

Flatbread
Kefir
Brown sugar

Break up desired amount of crisp flatbread in a wide mouthed soup bowl. Pour in a generous amount of kefir milk, and sprinkle with brown sugar.

KEFIR MILK DESSERT
(Melkeringer)

Melkeringer, a traditional summertime treat still used by those who love it's refreshing taste.

1 qt. lukewarm whole milk
½ cup kefir
½ cup sour cream
Cinnamon and sugar
Crushed zwieback

Bring milk to boiling point. Remove from heat and cool until lukewarm. Divide into 4 soup bowls and add 2 tablespoons each of kefir and sour cream to each bowl. Let stand covered at room temperature until firm. Refrigerate until serving time. Serve with cinnamon, sugar and crushed zwieback.

CREAM OF WHEAT PUDDING
(Semulepudding)

Cream of wheat pudding is surprisingly delicious, children and youth particularly enjoy it. It is a good way to get some nourishment into finicky eaters.

Cream of wheat, uncooked enough for 4 servings
Milk
Salt
2 tbsp. sugar
1 egg, large
1 tsp. almond extract
½ cup raisins
10 almonds, chopped fine
1 tsp. orange or lemon peel
Fruit sauce
Whipped cream, optional

In a heavy bottom utensil cook cream of wheat following direction on package, but substituting milk for water. When cooked add sugar. Remove from heat and stir in raisins and chopped nuts; then add slightly beaten egg, and return to heat, stirring constantly until it approaches the boiling point. Remove and add flavoring. Pour into dessert bowls. Sprinkle sugar on surface to prevent film from forming. If desired, pour the pudding into a large bowl rinsed with cold water and cool. Just before serving invert onto a platter, decorate with whipped cream and serve red fruit sauce or apricot sauce in a glass pitcher. If desired, the sauce may be poured directly over the pudding.

MILK DESSERT
(Opplagt melk)

    This old dessert recipe is known all across Norway. It was, in the old days, made from sour milk, which was hung in a cheesecloth to separate the whey. On one of my recent visits to Norway, however, I was served this dish and it was made with cottage cheese. Simple, quick and tasty.

1 cup cottage cheese
½ cup whipping cream
jello

    Follow package directions for your favorite berry jello. Mash the cottage cheese with a fork. Whip the cream and combine thoroughly with the cheese. Place in a clear dessert bowl and top with spoonful of your favorite berry jello. Pass sugar, milk, or cream.

CARAMEL PUDDING WITH EGGS
(Karamellpudding med egg)

    This is my very favorite Norwegian dessert. I never visit Norway without enjoying it at least once. It is easy to make, just read directions carefully, and the result will be perfect every time.

2 ½ cups milk or half and half
4 tbsp. sugar
½ vanilla bean,
    cut lengthwise or 2 tsp. vanilla sugar,
    or 2 tsp. pure vanilla extract
3-4 eggs

Caramel:
¾ cup water
¾ cup sugar

    Caramel pudding is made is usually from milk or cream, and eggs, and baked in a mold which has been coated with caramel. It is best to prepare the pudding a day in advance to allow for thorough chilling. It can be made in an oven-proof mold or in an oblong or round ovenproof pan of a size in proportion to the pudding recipe. The container can be completely filled as caramel pudding, if properly baked, will not rise. Use caution when working with caramel as it is extremely hot and if it comes in contact with any part of your body, a deep burn will result. DO NOT make caramel with small children underfoot.

Vanilla bean is by far the best flavoring, but vanilla sugar or extract can be used. If vanilla sugar or extract is used, add to the milk mixture last. If only cream is used, bring to a boil before adding vanilla bean. If the eggs are small, use more. If only cream is used, more eggs are required than with milk only.

In a heavy bottomed pan simmer half and half or milk, together with sugar and vanilla bean for 10 minutes. Cool to lukewarm and remove the vanilla bean. Thoroughly blend eggs, but do not over beat as this causes the pudding to become porous. Combine milk, or cream and eggs and strain through a sieve to remove any stringy parts of the egg yolks. Cool. Both the caramel and the egg mixture should be at room temperature. If the mixture is too hot it will melt some of the caramel and mix with the pudding and cause it to turn brown. Pour water into a smooth bottom cast iron skillet. When it boils add the sugar. Without stirring allow it to simmer until it turns a golden chestnut color.

As soon as sugar reaches the proper color, it should be a golden chestnut color and easy flowing, pour it into a pre-heated mold, (grip a pot holder in each hand) and tip and swirl the mold until bottom and sides are evenly coated, The caramel stiffens quickly, so work fast. Set the mold aside until caramel has completely hardened.

To steam the pudding, set mold in a pan with enough boiling water to reach half way up the sides of the mold, and place in a preheated 325 degree oven. During the steaming process the water should not boil or the pudding will rise and have air pockets. A small amount of pudding requires about 1 hour to bake, and larger amounts from 2 to 3 hours. To test for doneness lightly press surface with the back of a spoon. It should feel firm, yet elastic; or test with a toothpick - if it comes out clean the pudding is done. Remove from oven and chill.

To unmold, run a sharp knife around the edge and dip mold briefly in hot water. Place a platter on top and invert. The caramel has now melted to a sauce. A successful caramel pudding should be light and golden, shiny and velvet like. Use a decorator tube to glamorize it with "flowers" of whipped cream.

CARAMEL PUDDING WITHOUT EGGS
(Karamellpudding uten egg)

This pudding requires no baking. Make it in the morning, enjoy it in the evening.

2 cups milk
2 cups whipping cream
1 tsp. pure vanilla extract
2 tbsp. gelatin, unflavored

Caramel:
1 cup sugar
1 cup water

Bring the milk to a boil in a heavy bottom utensil, being careful not to scorch. Soften gelatin in a little water for 5 minutes. Add to milk. Whip cream with vanilla and add to the milk, and stir in 3 tablespoons of caramel.

Pour water in a heavy bottomed skillet. When it boils add sugar and simmer undisturbed until sugar turns a golden chestnut color and is easy flowing. Pour into a mold which has been rinsed with cold water, and quickly tip and swirl the mold until bottom and sides are evenly coated. Let harden before adding the creamy pudding. Refrigerate 3-4 hours. Just before serving invert onto a pretty glass dish. Decorate with whip cream "roses" if desired.

RUM PUDDING
(Rompudding)

2 eggs, separated
1/3 cup sugar
1 cup whipping cream
1 tbsp. gelatin, unflavored
1/2 cup hot water
2 tsp. rum extract or rum to taste

Beat egg yolks with sugar. Beat egg whites separately. Whip cream. Mix all together carefully and add rum extract. Soften gelatin in a little water for 5 minutes. Add enough boiling water to make 1/2 cup, making sure all gelatin is dissolved. Cool for about 10 minutes but do not allow to stiffen. Add to rum mixture and stir. Pour into mold which has been rinsed with cold water, and place in a refrigerator until it becomes firm. Garnish with whipped cream. Serve with red fruit sauce if desired.

RED FRUIT SAUCE
(Rød fruktsaus)

Red fruit sauce is the crowning glory to many a pudding such as rum pudding, cream of wheat pudding or rice cream. Make it from currant juice, cherry, strawberry or raspberry, they are all delicious.

2 cup juice of your choice
Sugar, if needed
1 tbsp. potato flour
Cold water

Bring juice to a boil. Meanwhile dissolve potato flour with a little water. Remove juice from heat and slowly add the potato flour thickening, stirring constantly to assure its smoothness. Bring quickly to a boil and remove from heat. If cooking period is prolonged the sauce may become thin or even elastic. The sauce should be smooth and not too thick. Pour sauce into a pitcher or other suitable container and sprinkle a little sugar over the top to prevent film from forming. Chill.

APRICOT SAUCE
(Aprikosesaus)

It was a real treat for us children when our Sunday dessert, was cream of wheat pudding topped with a red fruit sauce, or once in a great while this delectable apricot sauce.

1/4 cup apricots, dried
2 cups water
1/4 cup sugar
2 tbsp. potato flour

Rinse the apricots and let soak in the water for 3-4 hours. Let simmer in the same water until tender. Force through a sieve and let cool. Add sugar to taste, and potato flour. Pour back into the kettle and bring to a boil while constantly stirring. As soon as it begins to boil, remove from the heat and keep covered until cooled. Chill before serving.

SWEET FONDUE
(Søt fondue)

Friendships grow closer, and talk livelier around a fondue pot. This delightfully sweet, smooth sauce is great for dessert or an evening snack. If you are a *gjetost* fan, you will wish you could have this every night.

3 cups Ski-Queen goat cheese, diced
1 cup liquid or more, milk,
    cream, apple cider or orange juice
touch of cardamom, ginger
    cinnamon or nutmeg
Fresh fruit and bread sticks

Over moderate heat, melt the cheese while stirring continually. If sauce is too thin let sauce cook until liquid is reduced, or add a little cornstarch which has been stirred in a little water. Add your choice of spice if desired. Keep a low heat under the fondue pot. Arrange a tray of fruit and bread sticks for dipping. Be sure each person has a long fondue fork.

GOAT CHEESE DESSERT SAUCE
(Gjetost dessertsaus)

Making this sauce with Ski-Queen *Gjetost* will give a rich luscious golden sauce with a rich aroma. Remarkably good on ice cream as well as over pears and nectarines.

1 cup Ski-Queen goat cheese, grated
1/3 cup milk
1 tbs. honey or syrup
Touch of anise, cardamom, cinnamon or ginger

Over low heat melt the cheese with the milk and honey. Add your favorite seasoning.

WAFFLES
(Vaffler)

Norwegians love waffles! They bake the waffles in heartshaped cast iron waffle irons. You can use an electric iron, but some of us, spellbound by the traditional heartshaped irons, who believe foolishly, maybe, that Norwegian waffles, to taste their best, must be baked in the heartshaped irons.

Cakes and waffles baked in cast iron forms are among the oldest kind of Norwegian cakes. Some of the cake irons have been found with runic writings on them. The oldest waffle irons made one heartshaped or square waffle. Later three hearts in the same iron were popular. The heartshaped waffle iron in use today traditionally has five hearts.

Waffles may be enjoyed in the morning, at lunch time, or in the evening. They are great when unexpected guests come to your door, because, generally, we all have the simple ingredients on hand. And it is a comfort to know that something so flavorful does not cost much.

There are innumerable recipes for waffles in Norway, inexpensive and healthy lowfat ones, made with barley flour and without butter and cream. Crisp delectable ones are high in calories but nevertheless irresistible. Try delicious waffles made with yeast.

Some waffles you can serve with a variety of sandwich meats, others, you can make into cream cakes, or serve them with ice cream and berries. Or maybe you still prefer the more traditional way; buttered and sprinkled with sugar, or topped with a thick slice of the sweet Norwegian goat cheese, or a spoonful of your favorite berry jam.

In earlier times *HVERDAGSVAFLER*, everyday waffles, were made with barley flour (now available at health food stores). For guests the more refined flour was used with the addition of sour cream. The most commonly used waffle had a rather firm texture containing neither egg, yeast, nor baking powder, but boasted of better keeping qualities. The fancier waffle had fresh milk, cream, sour cream, butter, and sugar added which made a thicker and superior textured product.

Try several of these waffle recipes, and maybe, just maybe, you too will become an avid fan of the Norwegian waffles.

SOUR CREAM WAFFLES
(Rømmevafler)

1 ¾ cup flour
½ tsp salt
1 ⅓ cup sour cream
1 ⅓ cup water

In a medium sized bowl mix all ingredients until batter is smooth. Let rest about 30 minutes.

Heat a non-electric heartshaped, Norwegian waffle iron. It is ready for baking when it is so hot that a drop of water splatters when flipped across its surface. Lightly butter it's surface before the first waffle only. Pour about ¾ cup of the batter in the center of the iron, close the top and cook over direct heat until nice and golden on each side. Loosen waffle with a fork. Place the waffles on cake racks until completely cool. These waffles should be crisp.

SOUR CREAM WAFFLES II
(Rømmevafler II)

These waffles can be eaten hot or cold.
1 cup flour, sifted
1 tsp. baking soda
1 tsp. crushed cardamom
½ tsp. salt
2 eggs, separated
2 tbsp. sugar
¼ cup butter
2 cup sour cream
1 cup buttermilk

Sift together dry ingredients and set aside. Beat egg yolks and sugar until thick and lemon colored, about 10 minutes. Add melted butter gradually, followed by the sour cream and buttermilk. Beat until well blended. Add liquid mixture all at once to dry ingredients and mix until batter is smooth. Beat egg whites until they form peaks and gently fold into batter. Follow baking direction of Sour Cream Waffles I.

CRISP WAFFLES WITH CREAM
(Sprø kremvafler)

Delicious and quick to make. You may beat the egg whites separately to make them extra light, but it is not necessary.
1 ⅓ cup flour
½ tsp. salt
2 tbsp. sugar
1 tsp. vanilla sugar, or vanilla extract
⅓ cup, plus 1 tbsp. water
1 cup, less 1 tbsp. sour cream
½ cup butter, scant
3 egg

Mix all ingredients, except the egg whites, until you have a smooth batter. Let rest 25- 30 minutes. Beat egg whites until they form peaks and gently fold into batter. Follow baking directions for Sour Cream Waffles I. Place on cake racks until cool. Serve with berry jam or sprinkle with powdered sugar.

SOUR CREAM WAFFLES III
(Rømmevafler)

These appetizing waffles are best newly baked. Crisp on the outside and delicately tender on the inside. They are delicious hot or cold.

1 1/8 cup sour cream
3 1/3 cup flour
1/2 - 2/3 cup water, cold
1/2 tsp. salt
1 tsp. baking powder

Mix all ingredients together until batter is smooth. Let rest 10 minutes. Follow baking directions for Sour Cream Waffles I. Bake until golden brown, and let cool on cake rack.

EVERYDAY WAFFLES I
(Hverdagsvafler I)

Low in calories, inexpensive, and tasty. Bake in the afternoon, place in Ziplock bag, and enjoy as a treat following dinner. Recipe calls for cultured milk, (see Special Help Section) homogenized milk may be used but these waffles are tastier with cultured milk.

2 eggs
1 1/3 cup cultured milk
1 1/3 cup flour
1/2 tsp. baking powder
2 tbsp. sugar
3 tbsp. margarine, melted

Beat the eggs with half the milk. Mix dry ingredients and add to eggs, stir until batter is smooth. Add remaining milk and melted butter and mix well. Let batter stand 10 minutes. Follow baking directions for Sour Cream Waffles I. Serve with goat cheese or jam. Makes 8 heartshaped waffles.

EVERYDAY WAFFLES II
(Hverdagsvafler)

1 2/3 cup flour
1 1/2 tsp. baking powder
1 tbsp. sugar
pinch of salt

3 eggs, separated
1 2/3 cup milk (or cream)
3 tbsp. melted margarine or butter

Sift flour and measure. Beat egg yolks. Add milk and melted margarine. Combine dry ingredients and add to egg-milk mixture. Beat egg whites until stiff and fold into batter. If you use a non electric Norwegian waffle iron, heat it, ungreased, until a drop of water splatters when sprinkled on its surface. Pour about 1/3 cup of batter in center of hot iron.

Bake until golden brown and crisp (about 5 minutes). Serve with butter and goat cheese or tart jam.

CRISP WAFFLES WITH YEAST
(Sprø vafler med gjær)

The two following recipes are made with yeast. They are delicious, but both need time, up to 1 hour, to rise. This recipe is suitable for all kinds of sandwich toppings. The waffles are crisp and will stay crisp for a good while after cooled (do not pile on top of each other this will soften them) on a cake rack. In case they become soft you can heat them on a rack in the oven at a low temperature.

1 tbsp. yeast granules
1 1/3 cup milk, lukewarm
1 1/3 cup flour
1 tsp. sugar, if desired
pinch of salt
4 oz, plus 1 tbsp. butter, melted and cooled

Dissolve the yeast in the milk. Beat in the flour, sugar, and salt. Let rise 1 hour. Beat in the melted butter and pour the thin batter evenly across the hot waffle iron. If using a non electric Norwegian waffle iron, heat it until a drop of water sputters when sprinkled on its surface. Grease only once, before baking the first waffle. Bake until a nice dark brown color. If not well done, they will soon loose their crispness. Cool separately on cake racks. Approximately 10 waffles.

WAFFLES WITH YEAST
(Vafler med gjær)

If you are not in a hurry, these low fat waffles are incredibly delicious. The batter must be allowed to rise 1/2 of an hour. If they are baked too soon they will become too hard.

3 eggs
2-3 tbsp. sugar
2 cups milk, scant
2 tbsp. margarine, melted
1/2 cup water
1/2 cup sour cream
1 tbsp. yeast granules
Flour, about 2 1/4 cup

Beat eggs with sugar until light and fluffy 7 to 10 minutes. Add milk and melted margarine. Stir yeast into a little sour cream, and add with cup milk. Add enough flour to make the batter a proper consistency. Not too thin. Stir until well blended. Let stand and rise 3/4 of an hour until bubbles form. Do not bake too soon, this will make the waffles hard. Grease the iron well. Follow baking directions for Sour Cream Waffles I. Serve with butter and jam. These waffles taste just as good the next day if kept in an airtight plastic bag. They will loose their flavor somewhat if frozen.

SCRUMPTIOUS DESSERT WAFFLES
(Deilige dessertvafler)

These scrumptious waffles are a treat any time. Served with ice cream and fresh fruit, with a little sour cream and shredded milk chocolate or truffles, or layered as a cake with whipped cream and fruit. They may also be served plain with your favorite beverage, taking the place of cookies.

¾ cup Delfia Coco-fat*
⅓ cup sugar
1 tsp. rum flavoring and 1 tsp. pure vanilla extract
   or 2 tsp. vanilla sugar
pinch of salt
4 eggs
⅓ cup potato flour
1 ¾ cup flour
½ tsp. baking powder

Melt coconut butter, and cool slightly. Beat flavorings, sugar, and salt into the coconut butter until it foams. Beat in the eggs, one at a time. Combine flour and baking powder and add to egg mixture. Let rest 5 minutes. Follow baking directions for Sour Cream Waffles I. To keep them crisp, when removed from waffle iron place them singly on cake rack to cool. Stacking softens them. These waffles will keep well in an absolute airtight container for one month.*See Special Help Section.

BARLEY WAFFLES
(Byggmelsvafler)

2 ⅞ cup barley flour
1 ¼ cup flour, unbleached
1 tsp. salt
4 cups buttermilk
½ tsp. baking soda

Heat the waffle iron over low heat. Grease iron well with shortening or crackling. Spoon enough batter in the middle of the iron to make a full shaped waffle without overflowing. Bake on both sides until light brown.

LEMON WAFFLES
(Vafler med sitronsmak)

A rather unusual flavor, but very palatable. Taste wonderful served hot or cold.

5 eggs
¼ cup sugar
1 cup flour
1 tsp. lemon juice, fresh
½ tsp. lemon peel, freshly grated
1 cup sour cream
¼ cup butter, melted

Beat eggs and sugar until thick and fluffy, about 10 minutes. Alternately fold in the flour, which has been sifted with lemon peel. Add sour cream. Stir in the butter and lemon juice. Set batter aside to rest 10-15 minutes. Heat heartshaped waffle iron. It is hot enough when drops of water sprinkled on its surface sputter. Pour approximately ¾ cup batter in the center of the iron. Lower cover and bake until the steaming stops, 30- 60 seconds on each side. Do not peak during baking period. Makes 6 waffles.

Special Help Section

HARTSHORN SALT-Ammonium carbonate
(Hjortetakk)

At one time *hjortetakk* was made from deer antlers, but today it is chemically produced and can be purchased at a drug store as *AMMONIUM CARBONATE AQUA AMMONIAE or hartshorn salt*. It is also stocked by some Scandinavian Delicatessens. Hartshorn salt was the leavening agent used for use in cookies and crackers; it may leave a bitter taste in large cakes which contain a larger portion of moisture. Norwegian cookies, known for their crispness and delicate texture, owe some credit for these qualities to hartshorn salt. It should be kept in a tightly covered glass jar or it will quickly loose its effectiveness. It has a characteristic odor of ammonia which disappears during the cooking process.

SYRUP
(Sirup)

The syrup recommended in all recipes throughout this book, and which most closely resembles the syrup used in Norway, is a partially inverted refiner's syrup, such as Lyle's Golden Syrup, available at many supermarkets or at import delicatessens.

POTATO FLOUR
(Potesmel)

Potato flour is available form most Scandinavian delicatessens, health food stores, and now in many supermarkets. It is an excellent thickening agent for fruit soups, compotes, sauces and creams, and is also used in cookies and cakes.

When thickening small amounts of food it is preferable to combine the potato flour with whatever food is being thickened and stir while bringing it to a boil. Remove immediately as overcooking causes it to become elastic in nature, particularly in foods with high acidity. However, if the potato flour is not sufficiently cooked it will result in a raw floury taste. When preparing larger portions add the potato flour last. Blend potato flour with a little cold water. Bring food to a boil and remove from heat. Since the flour tends to settle at the bottom if allowed to stand, stir well before using. Slowly add the potato flour thickening while stirring constantly to assure smoothness. Bring quickly to a boil and remove from heat.

Anything thickened with potato flour should be cooled quickly. Sprinkle with a little sugar to prevent film from forming. When potato flour is used in breads and cakes it acts as a preservative and also results in a more moist product. When used for baking, substitute 5/8 cup of potato flour for 1 cup all purpose. As a thickening agent, substitute 1 1/2 teaspoons potato flour for 1 tablespoon all purpose flour.

KEFIR
(Kefir)

Kefir is a cultured milk product used in many traditional recipes. If you are unable to obtain unflavored kefir in your area, (check with your Natural Food Stores) you may obtain kefir culture (about $3.50 plus postage) by writing J-Vee Health and Diet Foods, 3720 Pacific Ave. S.E. Olympia, Wa. 98501 (206) 491-1930.*

BOILING MILK
(Koking av melk)

Some simple rules, to help you, through proper handling, to preserve the nutrients in the milk.

Keep milk refrigerated and well covered to prevent contamination, and the loss of vitamins by too much air intake.

Never boil milk for a long period of time. Too long of a cooking period will also reduce nutrients. When you use milk for rice porridge or other recipes requiring long cooking, boil the rice in water first.

When you boil milk, use a heavy bottom kettle. Avoid using an iron kettle unless it has a smooth bottom.

Stir occasionally as the milk is brought to a boil. Watch carefully so it does not boil over. Try not to use milk for boiling, direct from the refrigerator. It takes longer to boil and it then tends to scorch easily.

DELFIA COCO-FAT
(Delfia kokosmatfett)

Delfia coco-fat is similar to margarine in consistency, but with a totally different flavor. It is made from the oil of the coconut. Imported from Norway, it is available in 250 gram (8.8 oz.) packages, and costs about $2.10 plus postage. You can purchase it from most Scandinavian Delicatessens.* If your store does not carry this product, you may obtain it by writing or calling either of the following stores.:

Johnson Scandinavian Foods
2248 N.W. Market St.
Seattle, Wa. 98107.
(206) 783-8288

Scandinavian Specialty Prod.,Inc.
8539 15th Ave. N.W.
Seattle, Wa. 98117
(206) 784-7020

*No compensation whatsoever is received from recommending possible sources. It is hoped it will be a service to you.

TEMPERATURE CONVERSION TABLE
Temperatur Forvandling

Centigrade	Fahrenheit
63	145
71	160
93	200
100	212
107	225
110	230
121	250
135	275
140	284
149	300
160	320
163	325
177	350
180	356
190	375
200	390
205	400
210	410
218	425
220	428
225	437
232	450
246	475
260	500
274	525
288	550

To convert centigrade into fahrenheit: multiply by 9, divide by 5, add 32.

To convert fahrenheit into centigrade: subtract 32, multiply by 5, divide by 9.

WEIGHT AND MEASURES

Vekt og Mål
Equivalents

Deciliters	Cups	Grams	Ounces
0.56	1/4	25	0.87
0.75	1/3	30	1.0
1.13	1/2	50	1.75
1.5	2/3	75	2.63
1.68	3/4	80	2.8
2.27	1.00	85	3.0
2.83	1 1/4	100	3.5
3.0	1 1/3	125	4.4
3.4	1 1/2	150	5.25
3.75	1 2/3	200	7.00
4	1 3/4	300	10.05
4.5	2.0	400	14.00

1 deciliter equals 6 2/3 tablespoons.

Liquid Grams	Liquid Ounces	American Spoons/Cups
5	1/6	1 teaspoon (tsp.)
15	1/2	1 tablespoon (tbsp.)
100	3 1/2	6 2/3 tablespoons
227	8	1 cup (16 tbsp.)
250	8 1/2	1 cup plus 1 tbsp.
454	16 (1 pound)	2 cups (1 pint)
907	32	4 cups (1 quart)

Conversion Formulas: Norwegian, American, Metric

TO CONVERT	MULTIPLY	BY
Grams to ounces	The grams	0.035
Ounces to grams	The ounces	28.35
Liters to quarts	The liters	0.95
Quarts to liters	The quarts	1.057
Centimeters to inches	The centimeters	0.39
Inches to centimeters	The inches	2.54

CREDITS

Sources for photographs are:
Norwegian Dairies Association
   from
Ost & Fantasi   Photographs on page 33
Ostegleder   Photographs on page 33-34
   by Ruth Marcussen Kielland
Milkshake og Gamalost   Photographs on page 34
   by Ruth Marcussen Kielland
Some of the photographs in the above mentioned books were used for guidance in some of the illustrations in this book.

The following recipes, information, and sources are included in the Production of this book:

Ostegleder, *Ruth Marcussen Kielland*
   Gyldendal Norsk Forlag A/S
   Meierienes Prøvekjøkken, 1987
   Mountain Dairy Maid's Favorite, Jarlsberg Vegetable Soup, Jarlsberg Cod, Nøkkel Quiche, Nøkkelost Vegetable Casserole, Swiss Cheese and Green beans, Norvegia Filled Potatoes, Jarlsberg Filled Peppers, Norvegia Spinach Pie.

Milkshake og Gamalost, *Ruth Marcussen Kielland*
   Landbruksforlaget A/S
   Meierienes Prøvekjøkken, 1988
   Gamalost, Norwegian Swiss, Norvegia, Jarlsberg, Edam cheese, Nøkkelost, Ridder cheese, Tilsiter, Normanna, Goat cheese, Swiss or Norvegia Souffle, Summer cold Dish, Dessert Cheese.

Norwegian Dairies Associations Pamphlets:
   Nøkkelost Sauce, Game Sauce, Goat Cheese Gravy for Chicken or Game, Old Fashioned Sauce, Sour Cream Gravy, Nøkkel Omelette, Jarlsberg Vegetable Soup, Jarlsberg Filled Peppers, Goat Cheese Dessert Sauce, and Sweet Fondue.

Gammel Norsk Bondekost, Hefte II Ingrid Andersen:
   Sour Cream Porridge from Hardanger, Slåttegraut, A dairy Maid's Day, Travel to the Mountain Farm, from Hans Aansrud book, "Sidsel Sidserk".